DREAMWORKS® Shark Tale™

THE ESSENTIAL GUIDE

Oscar, a fish with a
wish to be famous

Lenny, a shark with
a heart of gold

Written by
Simon Jowett

DreamWorks® Shark Tale™

THE ESSENTIAL GUIDE

CONTENTS

OSCAR

O scar is a small fish with big dreams... and an even bigger mouth. He dreams of fame, fortune, a cool penthouse apartment, and a fin-tastic girlfriend. When he tells one great white lie, all his dreams come true at once... but will he stay alive long enough to enjoy it?

Fast mouth—good for talking himself into—and out of—trouble.

"SLAP ME SOME FIN!"

Washer-Fish

Oscar has worked at Reef City's Whale Wash for as long as he can remember. His moves make him the life and soul of the place—even if he doesn't always get to work on time. Luckily, kind-hearted Angie always clocks him in early.

Wrasse Facts

Home: Tropical waters
Size: 1–3 ft (30–90 cm) long
Food: Mollusks
Species: There are at least 600 species of wrasse

Fast fins—good for getting away from trouble he has just talked himself into!

In Too Deep

Oscar's in deep trouble—he doesn't have any money, his rent is due, and he owes Sykes, his short-tempered boss, five thousand clams! Oscar needs a miracle. What he gets is a tip for the big race... and a whole heap of trouble.

Sykes, Oscar's boss at the Whale Wash.

Sykes sends his jellyfish enforcers, Ernie and Bernie, to pull Oscar in for a chat. Using their powerful stingers, they show him it's time to pay.

(Not So) Lucky Day

Angie gives Oscar her grandmother's pearl to pay his debt to Sykes, but Oscar bets it all on a seahorse called Lucky Day! A win would make him a millionaire, but Oscar loses everything—and the story has just begun.

Oscar Lowdown

• Oscar may have the fastest mouth on the reef. It certainly gets him into trouble faster than any other fish!

• Oscar's the coolest dancer on the reef. He's always coming up with slick moves for his friends to copy. If he could, he'd dance with himself... but people would think that was weird!

• Oscar knows kung fu—well, the shouting and posing parts, anyway!

LENNY

L enny is a great white shark with a great big secret—he's a vegetarian. For years, he's kept this secret from his father, and for good reason, too. His father, Lino, is the ruthless head of the ruling shark elite. But now Lino wants Lenny and his brother Frankie to take over the Reef City operations. It's only a matter of time before Lenny's secret comes out!

When rumors about Lenny's secret reach Lino, he knows there's only one way to prove them wrong: Lenny must eat more than just the salad in his shrimp cocktail!

Finding Oscar

It was supposed to be Lenny's last chance to act like a real shark, but it was the beginning of the strangest friendship ever seen beneath the waves. Lenny should have eaten Oscar, but instead he set him free.

Lenny's coloring is good for hiding in the shadows of the kelp fields.

Bad Reputation

- Like Lenny, not all sharks are ferocious killing machines. Some of the largest sharks feed on the smallest creatures in the sea.

- The basking shark, the whale shark, and the megamouth shark are filter-feeders that live on zooplankton—tiny microorganisms that populate the oceans in vast numbers. The sharks gulp in huge amounts of sea water as they swim along and strain out the zooplankton.

Lenny and other great whites are the only sharks that can hold their heads up out of the water to look for prey.

"I CAN'T HELP IT. IT'S JUST THE WAY I AM."

Good eyesight—can spot ripe kelp from a hundred yards

Great White Facts

Home: Coastal temperate waters

Size: Up to 25 ft (7.5 m) long!

Fact: Great white sharks are the largest predatory fish in the world—and sometimes they attack humans.

Hiding With Da Homeboy

In hiding from the inhabitants of Reef City and from his own family, Lenny is able to be himself for the first time in his life. But as Oscar's reputation as the Sharkslayer grows, the time's coming when Lenny will have to act like a real shark again!

ANGIE

Angie is Oscar's one true love... or she would be, if Oscar would stop trying to be Somebody long enough to realize it! Angelfish by name and angel by nature, Angie has a big heart and—luckily for Oscar and Lenny—a weakness for hard-luck cases.

Sympathetic ear (for listening to Oscar's troubles).

Angie can eat all the doughnuts she wants and still stay slim and pancake-shaped!

Angie's stripes make her hard to see when she's hiding in weeds.

" DREAMS CAN BEGIN SMALL. YOU JUST HAVE TO START WITH A CLEAN SLATE "

Angie runs the Whale Wash office, taking calls and making sure that everything runs smoothly. She makes her job look a lot easier than it really is... as Ernie and Bernie find out when she goes missing.

Angelfish Facts

Size: Up to 6 in (15 cm) long

Food : Mostly vegetable matter

Fact: Angelfish are pancake-shaped. This allows them to spend the night tucked away from predators in narrow crevices in the reef.

Pretty Little Angel Eyes

• In her first-aid box, Angie keeps an all-purpose sea slug. The slug is great for cleaning wounds and reducing bruises... as long as the patient doesn't let it wander off.

• Angie hopes her grandmother's rare pink pearl will help Oscar to pay back Sykes... but Oscar's dreams may trip him up again...

• Angie's second-biggest weakness (after Oscar) is for doughnuts.

Angie can see through Oscar's tall tales.

Somebody One Day

Oscar is never a Nobody to Angie, even when his latest shrimp-brained scheme goes wrong. But when Oscar becomes Somebody and the whole reef thinks he's a hero, it looks like Angie has lost him for good!

The Truth?

Angie's the first of the Reef City fish to learn that the Sharkslayer's story is a sham—one set up with the help of Lenny the shark. Lenny lives in a store-room, but Angie's all for getting him out in the open—along with the painful truth. Oscar, however, has slippery plans of his own.

SYKES

Sykes the pufferfish is Oscar's boss at the Whale Wash. He's also Lino's main man in Reef City—or he was until Lino fired him. But Sykes isn't out for long; he's a fish with an eye for a profit, and when Oscar makes it big, he grabs a piece of the action.

"THERE'S NO SUCH THING AS A SURE THING."

Boss Sykes

Sykes doesn't like to be puffed. When things get too stressful, he takes time out to find his happy place. But when Oscar's involved, he can't help blowing up! At least, that's how it was when Oscar was short of cash...

Spikes make Puffer-Fish very hard to swallow!

Sykes calm and unpuffed

What's It To You?

• Sykes is very close to his mother— she calls him every day.

• There's only one way to Sykes's happy place: away from Oscar!

• Sykes wants people to realize that he's a nice guy... especially if they do what they're told!

Pufferfish Facts

Home: Tropical and subtropical seas

Size: Up to 20 in (50 cm) long

Fact: Pufferfish can expand because they have elastic skin and no ribs.

Females beware! Spikes are a pain when cuddling up to Sykes!

Small fins don't help much when puffed up

Elastic skin allows for expansion

When Oscar becomes the Sharkslayer, Sykes enjoys telling Lino what to do... but how long will the fun last?

13

ERNIE & BERNIE

The most chilled-out enforcers ever, Ernie and Bernie work for Sykes and use their stinging tentacles to extract money from any fish who owes their boss.

"CHILL, BRUTHA!"

Ernie thinks he's the better singer.

They both think they're the better dancer!

Tentacled Twins

Ernie and Bernie have worked for Sykes for as long as anyone can remember. They're always on hand to help their boss find his "happy place." If they were any more laid back, they'd be horizontal!

Jelly Fish Facts

Home: Coastal temperate water

Size: Bodies: 1–6 in (2.5–15 cm) long; up to 15 ft (4.5 m) long including tentacles!

Food: Plankton

Fact: Jellyfish spend part of their life stuck to a rock as something called a sessile or stationary polyp.

"RESPECT!"

Bernie thinks his hat's bigger.

"We Shocked Da Wrasse Fish"

Don't be fooled by Ernie and Bernie's "eazy" style—their floppy hats hide a mean streak a nautical mile wide. Just ask Oscar!

The brothers' stinging cells are called nematocysts.

Things look bad for Oscar when he tangles with Ernie and Bernie!

E & B's BOO-YA-KA BOX

• Reggae Boyz Ernie and Bernie don't like it when Oscar remixes their favorite song, "Don't Worry," in a hip-hop style.

• Their favorite video game is "Sharkslayer"—they love it when cyber-Oscar loses!

15

WHALE WASH

Where's a whale gonna go when he needs a wash, a wax, and a chance to wind down after a busy day? Sykes's Whale Wash, of course! The funky tunes and smooth moves are free—courtesy of Oscar and the Whale Wash crew!

Bungee crabs

Steam cleaner

Rinse hoop

Vacuum system

Angie's office

Scraper fish get busy here!

Soap dispenser— close your eyes!

Whale weigh station

Oscar's Crew

The Whale Wash workers are like a family— they're proud when Oscar becomes famous, and they're even happier when Oscar and Angie get together!

Wash Time

- You've got to have a sense of rhythm to work at the Whale Wash. It's a good thing Sykes owns it... 'cause with his two left fins, he'd never get a job there!

- The Whale Wash is powered by hot water from thermal vents in the reef—so it's totally eco-friendly.

Big sign for near-sighted whales

WHALE
WASH

Auto brush station

Turtles buff waxed whales here.

Locker room—scrape off the day's stink bubbles here!

WAX

Hot wax contains powdered mother of pearl

Poster of Sykes reminding his workers of the company motto—Cheaper and Faster!

Bubble blower—just for fun!

THE OFFICE

Angie's office is the nerve center of the Whale Wash. Angie answers the phone, checks in whales for a wash, wax, and barnacle peel, and still finds time to chat with their pilot fish. Even Ernie and Bernie (with four eyes, two mouths, and all those tentacles) can't run the Wash like Angie.

A Room With A View

But it's not all work in the office. It's here that Angie and friends watch Oscar's rise to fame—on the television above her desk. Thanks to resident sweetheart reporter Katie Current, all Oscar's antics are broadcast across the reef.

"Would you hold for a moment, please? Thanks, dog." Oscar creates some boogie-time with Angie!

LOLA

This super-fishal fin fatale always gets what she wants: Somebody to shower her with gifts, take her shopping till her fins drop off, and wrap her in the lap of luxury; then Somebody new to repeat the whole procedure.

"DEEP DOWN, I'M REALLY SUPERFICIAL."

Luscious lips for sweet-talking men out of their money

Swaying hips to hypnotize gullible male fish

Beware: poisonous spines!

Lionfish

Size: 1 ft (30 cm)

Food: Fish and crustaceans (shellfish)

Fact: The spines on a lionfish's dorsal fin are poisonous. Their sting is painful... and sometimes deadly!

After losing his chance with Lola at the racetrack, Oscar can't believe his luck when the fish of his dreams swims back into his fins!

Love Triangle

Angie can see that Lola doesn't care for Oscar, only for his money and fame. But when Angie sees them kissing, it looks like Oscar has made his choice.

On The Prowl

- At first, Lola believes Oscar's story that he's a high-roller. Then she discovers he's just a regular fish, and she's quick to dump him.

- But she's soon back on the scene when everybody thinks he's the Sharkslayer. Oscar's new penthouse is her kind of habitat!

- Rumor has it that she used to be a showgirl.

Powerful tail helps her change sides quickly

REEF CITY

Reef City... Coral Town... the Big Sea Cucumber... Here, every fish is small fry until they prove that they've got what it takes to stay afloat. It's sink or swim in Reef City, and it doesn't matter if you're a street urchin or the Big Kahuna— the city can make ya or break ya!

On The Streets

Oscar lives in a low-rent part of the reef... but even that is more than he can afford! He dreams of owning an apartment at the top of the sparkling coral towers, but has to be content hanging with small fry like Crazy Joe, a homeless Hermit Crab!

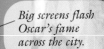

Big screens flash Oscar's fame across the city.

Crazy Joe—the local crackpot

Fan mail to Oscar here

Fire hydrant – rarely used underwater

The tops of coral towers are home to the city's elite.

Barnacle Bob's— Reef City's #1 dive

Guppy Gum—the city's favorite chew

Seahorse Show—events include obedience, agility, child-rearing (male sea horses only)

Streets are home to urchins, bottom-feeders... and Oscar!

LINO

Lino's the Codfather, the Shark of Sharks and undisputed Boss of Reef City. All other fish pay him respect, whether they're leopard sharks, hammerheads, killer whales, or swordfish. Lino's got big plans for his boys, Frankie and Lenny—little does he know what fate has in store for his whole operation.

Predator #1

Lino has worked hard to reach the top of the food chain in Reef City. He has protected his boys and raised them in the traditional shark way—eat first, ask questions later—and has done his best to ignore the rumors about Lenny. But the truth is about to come out... and it won't be pretty!

Lino's coloring camouflages him from above and below.

Sharks' fins help them to balance.

Great Whites

Food: Seals, dolphins, whales, tuna

Hobbies: Filling their gills with cool, rushing water

Fact: A great white shark's back teeth rotate forward when its front teeth are broken.

"IT'S A FISH-EAT-FISH WORLD."

Out And In

Sykes has been Lino's representative on the reef for a long, long time... but times are changing. Lino's putting Frankie and Lenny in charge and Sykes is out. The pufferfish just can't believe he's being told to blow.

Pet Piranhas

Lino keeps pet piranhas in his office. But don't be fooled by their wide grins—these little guys are just as deadly as their owner.

Lino keeps an eye on his Reef City operation.

Frankie's a messy eater, but Lino doesn't care. At least it's fish that Frankie's eating! Meanwhile, Lenny looks on in disgust—all he can do is weep for the fallen fish.

I'm The Boss!

• Lino has loved both his boys since they were small fry... but will he remember that when he discovers Lenny's secret?

• Lino dreams of retiring—maybe taking a trip up the coast to New England, where he hears the feeding's good.

FRANKIE

For as long as he can remember, Frankie's wanted to be a gangster. Lino's eldest son is a cold-hearted killer and a loyal son to Lino. He's the kind of shark every other great white can respect, and he wouldn't want it any other way.

"...NO BROTHER OF MINE COULD BE THIS PATHETIC!"

Feeding Time

Frankie hates fast food. He prefers his meals to stay still while he eats them.

"Fuhgeddaboutit, you're dead."

Who ordered the shrimp cocktail "to go"?

Great White Appetite

After a hard day getting heavy around the reef, Frankie loves to come home to a family meal. It doesn't matter who the family is—Frankie will make a meal of them! Frankie's philosophy is simple: if it moves, chomp it. If it don't move, chomp it till it does! No one has complained about it yet—but it's hard to argue from inside a great white!

Big Brutha

He may be a stone-cold killer, but Frankie's not all bad: he has kept Lenny's secret for years. He's a loyal brother, even if he doesn't understand why Lenny won't act like a real shark.

Thick skull, even for a great white!

Frankie has been known to eat the occasional surfboard.

Always ready to eat!

Frankie's top speed: 43 mph (69 km/h)

Badda-Bing!

• Frankie's hobbies include: eating... chasing speedboats... eating... scaring smaller fish.... eating... and eating!

• He's good at putting the strong-fin on his dad's enemies.

• His determination to show Lenny how a shark ought to behave is his undoing. If he hadn't been about to eat Oscar, the anchor would have missed him completely!

"BE A SHARK FOR ONCE!"

Listen to the Band

What could be better than live music to go with live food? This band can play anything from Italian opera to mambo... but all badly. However, no one's going to complain—the last fish to criticize their playing ended up as a drum skin and a new set of harp strings!

The baddest band on the seabed—literally!

Longnose waiter— happy to bring the bill

Red carpet—perfect for hiding blood stains!

LINO'S HQ

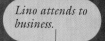

Lino attends to business.

Lino runs his operation from the wreck of an ocean liner that sits on the ocean floor outside Reef City. Lino hasn't changed much about the place since he moved in, and he's now so powerful that he rarely leaves. Let's go through the porthole and take a closer look...

Lino's Office

The office is the core of Lino's operations. Containing his books, records, and piranhas, it's where Lino is most at home.

Dining Room

If Lino invites you to dinner, it's always smart to ask if you're going to be a guest... or the dish of the day! Lenny's vegetarianism is exposed when he frees the shrimp cocktail.

Luca has eight tentacles...

... and each tentacle has 240 suckers...

... which is over 1,900 suckers!

LUCA

Luca is Lino's trusted advisor, or consigliere. Inside his bulbous brain, Luca carries details of Lino's operations and has his tentacles in lots of pies. The brains behind Angie's kidnapping, he is a sinister presence in the shadows... and when there aren't enough shadows, he has enough ink to make his own!

Slick Squid

• Luca takes care of Lino's collection of opera records. It's important to set the right tone for a meeting.

• It's Luca's job to take note of Lino's latest plans... which isn't easy when he keeps losing your pen!

• Like other octopuses, if Luca lost an arm he could grow another one back—but it's not something he wants to try in a hurry!

Watch Out, Sucker!

Whenever Lino wants something done that's low-down, underhand, and just plain sneaky, he always sends for his eight-armed accomplice!

Eight-Bar Blues

When he's not running errands for Lino, Luca likes to play the piano in the ballroom of the wrecked ocean liner. When he retires, he'd like to open a small piano bar in Reef City's Green Light District.

Octopus Facts

Size: 24–36 in (60–90 cm) long

Fact: Octopuses use an inky liquid to trick unsuspecting enemies.

Luca has no nose—a good thing, since he has eight armpits!

THE FIVE FAMILIES

The Five Families run the reef. No one family could stand up against the other four—that's the way it's always been, and tradition is very important to these fish. If a "situation" arises, they meet to chew over the problem... sometimes literally!

The Great Whites

Top of the food chain, the great whites are respected for their strength and ruthlessness. Lino has run the families and the reef for years—until the Sharkslayer appears and starts shaking things up.

Killer Whales

They ain't sharks—they ain't even fish!—but their fearsome strength and love of the hunt have earned them the respect of the other families.

Swordfish

These sharp-tempered fish are always ready for a fight. Their tough-guy reputation is let down when they catch a cold or sniffle—it ain't easy wiping a nose that long!

Leopard Sharks

They might be sharp dressers and music-lovers, but they're not sissies! Young leopard sharks take pride in their appearance and work hard to earn their stripes. Don Feinberg is one of Lino's oldest friends.

Hammerheads

Why go around an obstacle when you can go through it? The hammerheads have a tendency to rush in without thinking and often can't see what's right in front of their faces.

RACE DAY

Oscar goes to the racetrack to find Sykes and pay back the five thousand clams he owes him... but a hot tip burns a hole in Oscar's resolve, and he bets all his clams on the seahorse Lucky Day. This bet causes ripples that reach way beyond the reef.

Lucky Day makes his break here.

Warm-up track

Can't Lose?

After a bad start, Lucky Day races around the track and takes the lead. Oscar and Sykes watch the race from the VIF (Very Important Fish) room, and they are already counting their winnings as the plucky seahorse approaches the finish line...

Oscar thinks he's winning, and for some of the race, he is—then Lucky Day takes a fall!

Lucky Day falls here.

Finish line— Oscar certainly looks finished!

Small dorsal fins beat almost as fast as a hummingbird's wings!

Sea Biscuit powers into the lead.

Seahorse Facts
Size: 2–8 in (5–20 cm)

Food: Small marine creatures such as larvae

Fact: Daddy seahorses are the only males that give birth to their young!

Salmonella struggles to reach Candy Cane and Fish Fingers.

Lucky Day lags behind.

Starting gates

Huge monitor for watching the race

Faulty gate delays Lucky Day—Oscar can hardly look.

Crash barrier

THE GREAT WHITE LIE

After losing his money on Lucky Day, Oscar is on the receiving end of some high-voltage payback courtesy of Bernie and Ernie. Then Frankie and Lenny appear... and Oscar's in danger of becoming the vegetarian shark's first fish dish!

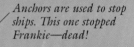

Anchors are used to stop ships. This one stopped Frankie—dead!

Last Words

Lenny's inconsolable, but Frankie's last words are for his loving brother: "You are such... a moron!" Then Frankie, like every good mobster, "sleeps with the fishes."

Frankie never knew what hit him.

By the time the silt has settled, things will never be the same again.

Birth Of A Legend

Oscar has no idea where the anchor that saved his life came from... but he's not about to complain! Grief-stricken Lenny runs away, leaving Oscar with one dead shark and an opportunity too good to miss!

Ernie and Bernie flee at the sight of Frankie—then, moments later, they see him at Oscar's feet. They put two and two together, and the legend of the Sharkslayer is born!

Lenny feels so guilty about Frankie's death that he runs for cover.

THE BIG KAHUNA

O scar returns to the city with a cool new reputation and a name to go with it: Sharkslayer! Everybody wants to be his friend, and the money and the deals flood in. It's Oscar's dream come true—at last, he's a Somebody. King of the City. The Big Kahuna. And the Big K can't be living in a one-room apartment—he belongs at the top of the reef!

Casa de Oscar

Top a' the reef, Ma! This penthouse apartment is Oscar's dream come true. A prime piece of reef real estate, it has everything a young fish on the make needs... and it's Oscar's, thanks to one great white lie.

Modern art on walls

The only game on Oscar's console is "Sharkslayer"!

House Party

As soon as Oscar moves in, the party starts! Suddenly Oscar's got a whole new gang: Sykes, Ernie and Bernie, Crazy Joe, and Lola want to know him. The joint is jumping, but Oscar's waiting for the one fish he really wants to see—Angie.

Suddenly everybody wants a piece of Oscar—especially Sykes, who steps in to manage the Sharkslayer.

Air-filled sofa cushions—perfect for relaxing after a long day's... relaxing!

FAKIN' IT

Crazy Joe

Lino's sharks are moving in on Reef City; their target: the Sharkslayer. Oscar's got to find a way to fend them off or he's going to be fish paste by suppertime. The plan he comes up with is crazier than Crazy Joe...

Oscar needs people to think he has killed another shark. Lenny has a talent for the dramatic. The great white lie is about to get even bigger...

An Oscar-Winning Performance

Oscar and Lenny ham it up—Lenny plays the Evil Shark and Oscar plays the Sharkslayer. If their plan works, Oscar's reputation will be bigger than ever. If it fails, the whole of Reef City will see it happen.

Sykes doesn't want to see Oscar get chomped because he hates to lose... especially money!

41

FIN

Fish of the Year

Y OO

pull out section

reporter Guppy

with Whitebait page 3

PlanktonPlay

grand wrasse oscar

Oscar the

Reef City is reeling with g news of the phenomenal rise of Oscar if the lowly h worker to superhero status in his Whale one-fish to protect he world ar fishes Sharks

I know Fin-Fu

"And I was all like, you're gonna come at me like that? You're gonna come at the 'O' like that?" In a flurry of fast-fin action, Oscar demonstrates how he brought down the Great White that some are claiming was none other than the eldest son of

Oh, er.... hello
Super Oscar

?

EANIC

20 Clams

Health Fin rot guide
Business Mr. Fifty Percent:
Sykes' self-inflating success story!

Sharkslayer!

Reef City Goes Oscar Crazy!

"Who da man?" Reef City knows: Oscar the Shark-slayer has been the fish of the moment, ever since he single-handedly 'put the hard fin' on a marauding Great White. The reef has been in a state of excitement since the news broke, but Oscar has been taking it all in his stride. "Ain't no big thing," he told this reporter over the phone from his new penthouse apartment. "I just went out there – completely o my lonesome, you understa

THE JAWFUL TRUTH

Hiding out in the storeroom at the Whale Wash, Lenny shares his secret with Oscar. Oscar has a secret or two of his own... and one of them's Lenny! Oscar's no shark-slayer, Lenny's no man-eater, and they're both in big trouble if their secrets get out!

You Can't Handle the Truth!

Angie's surprised to discover that, along with bottles of detergent, wax for the turtles, and extra Barnacle Peel and Seaweed Wrap, the store room at the Whale Wash also contains A GREAT WHITE SHARK! Terrified at first, she soon discovers the truth—that Lenny's a secret friend.

Oscar learns Fin-Fu to help him be the Sharkslayer.

Lenny's happy lying low in the storeroom, but Angie knows this white lie's too big for people not to notice!

What Next?

Oscar knows Angie's answer to their problem—"Tell the truth!"—but he doesn't want to hear it. Lino's sharks would tear him apart... assuming they got to him before Sykes, Ernie, Bernie, and the rest of Reef City!

Lenny loves the idea that Oscar's the Sharkslayer. How dumb are folks on the reef?! Still, he's good at playing his role—and keeping a straightish face!

FiN-ALE

Everything falls apart when Lino kidnaps Angie. It's up to Oscar, Sykes, and their new friend Sebastian the Dolphin (a.k.a. Lenny) to confront Lino and the rest of the Five Families. The sit-down turns ugly when Sebastian's true identity is revealed; and the chase is on... to the Whale Wash!

Lino wants to know the truth about the Sharkslayer... but he also learns the truth about Lenny. Will he turn his back on his only remaining son?

Group Hug

Sykes realizes that this is the first time he has ever helped anyone without first working out his percentage. He's so moved that he gives Ernie and Bernie a group hug... and all three of them get a shock!

Lenny's happy to head home with his dad. He has big plans to brighten up that dingy old wreck!

True Love

When the suds settle, will Oscar realize that he's always been a Somebody—to Angie?

Life After "Shark Tale"

• Luca retired from the mob and opened a piano bar. Patrons love his music—especially that eight-arm style!

• Lola moved in with Don Feinberg. She made him very happy, at least as long as his money (and heart) lasted.

• Crazy Joe went into real estate and now sells sea shells on the sea shore.

LONDON, NEW YORK, MUNICH,
MELBOURNE, AND DELHI

ART EDITOR Guy Harvey   **SENIOR EDITOR** Andrew Szudek

ART DIRECTOR Mark Richards   **PUBLISHING MANAGER** Cynthia O'Neill Collins

DTP DESIGNER Dean Scholey   **CATEGORY PUBLISHER** Alex Kirkham

PRODUCTION Nicola Torode

First American Edition, 2004
Published in the United States by
DK Publishing, Inc., 375 Hudson Street,
New York, New York 10014
04 05 06 07 08 10 9 8 7 6 5 4 3 2 1

A Cataloging-in-Publication record for this book is available from the Library of Congress.

ISBN 0-7566-0552-0

Reproduced by Media Development and Printing Ltd, U.K.
Printed and bound in the United States by R. R. Donnelley & Sons.

Acknowledgments

DK Publishing would like to thank:
Kristy Cox, Corinne Combs, Rhion Magee and the staff at DreamWorks L.L.C.;
Roger Harris for additional artworks.

Discover more at
www.dk.com